OVE

"And Noah lived after the flood three hundred and fifty years." Genesis 9:28

This book recounts the flood story of The Apostolic Church of Lafayette, and how a catastrophic, God-ordained flood experience, and a series of miracles over the span of seven years thereafter, allowed the church to move from its former location to a world-class, beautiful facility…with a boulevard. This book addresses how the boulevard and so many other details would be central to the flood story and evidence of just how faithful God is to the prayers and work of the elders.

Just as Noah lived 350 years after the flood in his day, so we too are living life fruitfully and abundantly after the flood of our day. This is our story, and we share it with you for the glory of God Almighty. He Brought Us Up!

II

THE ONLY BIBLE PLAN OF SALVATION

"Then Peter said unto them, Repent, and be baptized every one of you in the name of Jesus Christ for the remission of sins, and ye shall receive the gift of the Holy Ghost."
Acts 2:38

He Brought Us Up

Written by
Pastor Steven D. Schwing, Sr. and
Shane J. Milazzo

Contributions and edits by:
Rebecca Schwing
Jessica Roy

Lafayette, Louisiana U.S.A.

Copyright 2025; All Rights Reserved

Amazon Kindle Self-Publishing

Visit lafayetteac.org for orders and information

DEDICATION

*This book is dedicated to those saints who, like the
priests of old, have carried the church on
their shoulders throughout this whole ordeal.
Though it was a sacrifice and was not easy at times,
you stuck with it.*

May God bless you for your love and loyalty.

Sincerely,

Pastor Schwing

TABLE OF CONTENTS

Overview of Book	i
Dedication	vii
Foreword	3
About the Writers	7
He Brought Us Up	11
Prelude	15
Timeline	18
The Miracles	25
Chapter 1	27
Chapter 2	31
Chapter 3	35
Chapter 4	45
Photos	97
Chapter 5	149
Chapter 6	163
Conclusion	169

FOREWORD

By Pastor Jeffrey Heard, Sr.
Carencro, Louisiana

In the work of God, it is easy in the present time to see what God has done, but in the past, when God was doing that work, it was not always easy to know exactly what He was working toward. Like a page of unconnected dots, we experience the individual events yet fail to see the larger picture until it is finished. A wise man will carefully follow the instructions of 1 Corinthians 4:5 and "...*judge nothing before the time*..." for one just never knows what God might do.

As to the Rev. John H. Broussard, a couple of words come to mind. One word is independent: As in all by himself. He and his wife, Sis. Helen Broussard, began their work for God with basically no help and not even much encouragement. Another word I would associate with Rev. John H. Broussard is "spiritual," meaning a tangible manifestation of the Spirit of God. He and his wife made many sacrifices with the expectation of seeing the Spirit of

God made tangible in the lives of those who would attend their church.

We can see in his conversion the gem of his ministry as he received a dramatic experience of the Holy Ghost at a tent meeting he did not even intend to attend. Just as he sat down, without any music, preaching or instruction, he was quickly affected by the Spirit of God, began to repent and very soon stood up and began to speak in other tongues so loudly that he was heard all across a very large congregation.

The mission of the Rev. John H. Broussard was that any and all would have this same experience and that they would then serve the Lord with all of their hearts and be found faithful. None of this, in his mind, required anything fancy or highfalutin. Fancy preaching, fancy clothes, fancy singing, and fancy buildings were all distractions. What people needed was a real experience with God by receiving the Holy Ghost with the evidence of speaking in tongues. This experience changed his life, and he believed it would change the lives of any who had it, and this would, in his mind, remain the focus of his church. This was his vision and in retrospect it is easy to see that it is what drove him in his work.

Sis. Broussard shared her husband's vision completely but probably had a greater desire to see their tremendous work represented in a more fitting, visible display. She prayed for years for a beautiful church on a grand boulevard as a witness to the great work they were doing. Home mission works tend not to produce the kind of finances that could support this kind of dream, but she dreamed of it and prayed for it anyway. In looking back, she also obviously had a vision that pressed her continually forward.

In the following pages, Bro. Schwing tells the story and provides many details of how all this calling and all this vision came into fruition. This writer witnessed the manifestation of this vision in real-time, as did many others, and what can now be said is that Bro. Schwing never wavered. In this long, arduous process, what stands out most is that for every door that was opened, it merely led to another three that were closed and yet, Bro. Schwing remained confident year after year, cancellation after cancellation, interruption after interruption, and always positively pressing forward.

In hindsight, it is obvious that he also had a part in this calling and this vision and pressed onward in the work and the will of God. This was the realization of a multi-generational vision brought about through much prayer and labor. Surely it was not easy, but God was going to do this, and He has done it. Congratulations Bro. and Sis. Schwing and this church congregation on a job very well done.

ABOUT THE WRITERS

Pastor Steven D. Schwing, Sr.

Pastor Steven D. Schwing, Sr., was born and raised in New Iberia, Louisiana, and has been a member of The Apostolic Church of Lafayette since 1989. He was ordained into the ministry in 1995 by the late Rev. John H. Broussard, and he became pastor in January 2000.

Before his born-again experience (Acts 2:38), he graduated from Christ for the Nations Theological Seminary in Dallas, Texas, and he continued to study for a time at the University of Southwestern Louisiana.

He was the owner of S.D. Schwing Electric, Inc., prior to being pastor of the church. Ownership of the company was transferred in 2000 and it is still in operation. He is a singer/songwriter/musician, a skilled carpenter, a seasoned outdoorsman, and an accomplished cook.

Having been pastor of the church for a quarter of century, he has preached locally, domestically, and internationally, and has been a supporter of home missions and foreign missions works abroad. He is a friend and mentor to many Apostolic brethren throughout the world. He is a contender of the faith, a servant-leader, and a man who both preaches and lives a life of prayer, holiness, and consecration. His vision of loving God and loving one's neighbor as oneself permeate his ministry.

He has been married to his high school sweetheart and love of his life, Mrs. Rebecca Schwing, for 36 years. He is the father of three sons and one daughter, and the grandfather of seven grandchildren.

Bro. Shane J. Milazzo

Bro. Shane J. Milazzo was born in New Iberia, Louisiana and raised in Lafayette, Louisiana. He has been a member of The Apostolic Church of Lafayette since 1996, and was ordained into the ministry by Pastor S.D. Schwing, Sr. in 2007. He is a graduate of the University of Southwestern Louisiana, the University of Louisiana at Lafayette, the University of West Florida's Teacher Ready educator licensure program, and the American College of Education.

He has served as principal of Apostolic Christian School since 2007, and as director of Eagle's Nest Daycare and Preschool since 2022 wherein he has a dual role as a licensed Louisiana Pathways early childhood instructor. He serves as Bible study teacher and coordinator, and as Spanish outreach director. He studied Spanish through classes and language-cultural immersion school in Central and South America, and he has been privileged to travel and contribute to foreign mission works throughout the world.

In 2008, he earned his statewide jurisdiction notarial commission under Louisiana's unique Civil Code

Napoleonic system. Several years later, he founded iNotaryNow, a notarial educational solutions company. He sold the company in 2024 and now serves as instructor and materials writer for the company and as adjunct faculty for several educational institutions. He has written several books, and he enjoys playing traditional fingerstyle arrangements on any acoustic guitar (especially on C.F. Martins)!

He has been married to his high school sweetheart, Mrs. Maria Milazzo, for nearly 26 years, and they have a son and daughter, both of whom they adopted from Guatemala.

HE BROUGHT US UP

*Joshua 24:17 "For the LORD our God, **he it is that brought us up…"***

Psalms 97:1 "The LORD reigneth; let the earth rejoice; let the multitude of isles be glad thereof."

Proverbs 13:22 "A good man leaveth an inheritance to his children's children: and the wealth of the sinner is laid up for the just."

Isaiah 52:7 "How beautiful upon the mountains are the feet of him that bringeth good tidings, that publisheth peace; that bringeth good tidings of good, that publisheth salvation; that saith unto Zion, Thy God reigneth!"

Revelation 19:6 "And I heard as it were the voice of a great multitude, and as the voice of many waters, and as the voice of mighty thunderings, saying, Alleluia: for the Lord God omnipotent reigneth…"

God's Use of Nature and Governments to Accomplish His Will Permeate the Bible
Ezra 6: 7-10, 14

"<u>Let the work of this house of God alone; let the governor of the Jews and the elders of the Jews build this house of God in his place.</u> *Moreover I make a decree what ye shall do to the elders of these Jews for the building of this house of God:* <u>that of the king's goods, even of the tribute beyond the river, forthwith expenses be given unto these men, that they be not hindered.</u> *And that which they have need of, both young bullocks, and rams, and lambs, for the burnt offerings of the God of heaven, wheat, salt, wine, and oil, according to the appointment of the priests which are at Jerusalem,* <u>let it be given them day by day without fail:</u> *That they may offer sacrifices of sweet savours unto the God of heaven, and pray for the life of the king, and of his sons...* <u>And the elders of the Jews builded, and they prospered through the prophesying of Haggai the prophet and Zechariah the son of Iddo. And they builded, and finished it, according to the commandment of the God of Israel, and according to the commandment of Cyrus, and Darius, and Artaxerxes king of Persia.</u>"

Ezra 7: 12-21

"Artaxerxes, king of kings, unto Ezra the priest, a scribe of the law of the God of heaven, perfect peace, and at such a time. I make a decree, that all they of the people of Israel, and of his priests and Levites, in my realm, which are minded of their own freewill to go up to Jerusalem, go with thee. Forasmuch as thou art sent of the king, and of his seven counsellors, to enquire concerning Judah and Jerusalem, according to the law of thy God which is in thine hand; <u>And to carry the silver and gold, which the king and his counsellors have freely offered unto the God of Israel, whose habitation is in Jerusalem, And all the silver and gold that thou canst find in all the province of Babylon, with the freewill offering of the people, and of the priests, offering willingly for the house of their God which is in Jerusalem: That thou mayest buy speedily with this money</u> bullocks, rams, lambs, with their meat offerings and their drink offerings, and offer them upon the altar of the house of your God which is in Jerusalem. And whatsoever shall seem good to thee, and to thy brethren, <u>to do with the rest of the silver and the gold, that do after the will of your God. The vessels also that are given thee for the service of the house of thy God, those deliver thou before the God of</u>

Jerusalem. And whatsoever more shall be needful for the house of thy God, which thou shalt have occasion to bestow, bestow it out of the king's treasure house. And I, even I Artaxerxes the king, do make a decree to *all the treasurers which are beyond the river*, that whatsoever Ezra the priest, the scribe of the law of the God of heaven, shall require of you, *it be done speedily*…"

PRELUDE

It was in 1971 on a seemingly insignificant street in Lafayette, Louisiana called Lana Drive, in a small wood-frame house, that The Apostolic Church of Lafayette (ACL) began in a living room with one 14-year-old boy. God's hand was clearly upon Rev. John H. Broussard (affectionately and respectfully known as Bro. Broussard to all) and his wife, Sis Broussard, as they began to reach the lost. One of the very first lessons that God was going to teach them was that one soul is worth more than the whole world. Each person that came to church was another opportunity for them to give of themselves for that one life. It was with this attitude and spirit that our church was built. Humility and servanthood were the hallmarks of every convert.

Every Saturday, the blossoming congregation would knock on doors and bring the good news to Lafayette and surrounding cities. Buses and vans were purchased to bring visitors every week. God was pleased and He blessed the work. Through every trial, there was always victory and promise.

The church grew and added onto the little house; eventually outgrowing its original Lana Drive location, the church purchased a piece of property on "Doc" Duhon Road. At first, a horse stable was converted into the nursery and the barn into the sanctuary. Afterwards, a new sanctuary was built and again, it was outgrown in a few years. A third sanctuary was built in the early 1980s.

From its inception, the story of ACL is filled with miracles of God's provision! Along with these blessings, God gave the church many promises about the future. No doubt, we are here today enjoying the benefits of the foundation that was laid by the elders!

Just as the church in the wilderness, God has led us to the land of promise flowing with milk and honey. This is our story! From a few days before the flood of 2016 to this day, we stand in awe of what God has done!

We will endeavor to tell our story by presenting a string of miracles. As Daniel 4:3 declares, "*How great are his signs! and how mighty are his wonders! his kingdom is an everlasting kingdom, and his dominion is from generation to generation."*

Since the beginning of man's existence, in the act of salvation, and in everyday life, the Lord has always been involved in the affairs of men, sometimes in silence and obscurity, and sometimes for all to see and hear. This involvement stems from His interest and love for mankind. His miracles span from the simplest of things that sometimes go unnoticed to the extraordinary things that are altogether overwhelming to comprehend. The stories of all the heroes of faith would tell us how capable God is, how wise He is, how loving He is, and how faithful He is.

Our story is a testimony of the same. Our new campus and magnificent buildings on Town Center Parkway stand as a testament to the greatness of our God.

TIMELINE OVERVIEW

The immediate flood story spans seven years. An overview of the general timeline is as follows:

~2016~

August 12th and 13th—The Great Flood. Services were held in our sister work's facilities in Carencro for three months until enough repairs were done at Duhon Road for us to have church in our own building.

September 15th—School began in the fellowship hall. Walls were built and we divided classes as small as permissible so that we would have a place for instruction.

November—We began to congregate in the partially repaired sanctuary again.

~2017~

The long year—During all of 2017, we remained in the sanctuary for church and the fellowship hall for school.

~2018~

The first part of the year continued to be difficult and slow.

Late April/early May—A geo-study assessing the slabs and underlying ground/soil was conducted.

June—A devastating geo-study report was issued by engineers effectively condemning the sanctuary and the fellowship hall. The engineers determined that there were cavities and areas of wash-out both in and under the foundations caused by the floods. The engineers recommended, and insisted upon, immediate evacuation of the buildings.

July—Substantial damage determinations were issued by the local government for our slab buildings. The pier-buildings had already been declared substantially damaged. We went back to Carencro for four months but this time, there was nothing to come back to since all our buildings were deemed uninhabitable.

Later in July— "THE" FEMA and GOHSEP meeting. This meeting was a true turning point after working through the flood situation for nearly two years.

September—We began school in a temporary campus provided by FEMA in "butler-building" classes. Little did we know how important that would be in the future.

October—We were awarded a grant for permanent work reconstruction. That grant was massive. Hallelujah!

November—We began congregating in a large tent, complete with air conditioning and heating, as part of our temporary campus. Sound became a problem with the adjacent neighborhood. This situation lasted for over 3 ½ years.

~2019~

January—A new piece of property was purchased at Town Center Parkway far above the floodplain; the property was originally going to be the clubhouse for a proposed golf course.

February—Requests for qualifications for architects went out; this process had to be repeated.

June—Requests for proposal for contractors went out; there were delays given various requirements, etc.

October—A contractor was chosen, but there were more delays in preparing for preconstruction earthwork given inclement weather and logistics.

November—We held our ground-breaking ceremony with an anticipated building completion date of August 2021, but there were more delays with weather, logistics, and deploying equipment.

~2020~

January—Building was slated to begin but heavy rain caused additional delays. It was entirely too wet and muddy to begin.

February/March—The Covid19 pandemic began. Work effectively stopped.

May—Work slowly resumed as pandemic shutdowns eased somewhat.

August—Hurricane Laura; the tent was destroyed and had to be rebuilt.

September—Hurricane Delta; the tent was destroyed again and had to be rebuilt.

~2021~

We experienced delays and slow progress with the buildings the entire year post-Covid19. Materials were constantly back-ordered, human resources were challenging to find, and the list of issues we encountered continued. Nevertheless, God was in all the delays and all the waiting. He had a plan!

~2022~

We experienced more delays during the first part of the year.

June—We had our first service in the new fellowship hall (named Broussard Hall in honor of Bro. and Sis. Broussard) at Town Center Parkway. We continued to have services in the fellowship hall for a year while construction on the sanctuary slowly progressed.

June—We had graduation in our new buildings. The Class of 2022 was in the temporary campus at Duhon Road during the entirety of their high school years.

August—We had our first day of school in the new facility. It was amazing!

~2023~

August 13th—Seven years to the day of the flood, we had our first service in the new sanctuary. The experience of that first service is very hard to describe. After seven years—to the day—we were finally in our new and beautiful sanctuary.

~2024~

The work continued in that we added a fountain in the front of the property, we had a lawn shed built, we added a large storage room to Broussard Hall, we continued working on building out our Sunday school classes, we completed the beautiful spiral staircase in the sanctuary foyer, and we prepared the sanctuary balcony for occupancy.

~2025~

February 5th-7th—Our Grand Opening, which is when this publication was officially distributed for the first time.

OVERVIEW OF MIRACLES
THE DETAILS OF EACH MIRACLE ARE REHEARSED AS THE BOOK PROGRESSES

- Miracle 1: The floodway
- Miracle 2: The school and its registered status with the state
- Miracle 3: The flood itself
- Miracle 4: The flood is made an official Federal Emergency Management Agency (FEMA) disaster with grant funds available
- Miracle 5: House of Worship (HOW) Memo
- Miracle 6: "THE" meeting
- Miracle 7: The TESI (sceptic) tap
- Miracle 8: Disaster Relief Recovery Act
- Miracle 9: Property at Town Center Parkway
- Miracle 10: FEMA approves property at Town Center Parkway
- Miracle 11: Covid19 and the school's contingency plan
- Miracle 12: Temporary campus meets all Louisiana Department of Education Covid19 requirements

- Miracle 13: Vetting our architectural and engineering (A&E) firm
- Miracle 14: Bidding and construction at Town Center Parkway begin before inflation and Covid19
- Miracle 15: First service at Town Center / August 13th, 2023—Seven years to the day of the flood!
- Miracle 16: The boulevard which was an answered prayer even after Sis. Broussard had passed away…a testimony of God's faithfulness
- Miracle 17: The miracle of giving

There are over a dozen more miracles that are of a sensitive, financial, and/or personal nature in some way; several miracles are also difficult to convey and to address given the context of them and various other details. That all said, there are over 30 documented miracles recorded in this flood story, and we have chosen to share some of those as a testament to God's faithfulness. God powerfully, demonstrably, and overwhelmingly moved on our behalf as *"He Brought Us Up!"*

CHAPTER 1

THE DREAM

John 14:29 "And now I have told you before it come to pass, that, when it is come to pass, ye might believe."

It all started with a dream; it was a message from God to me that the events that were about to transpire were all in His plan.

In the dream, I was in front of our old church on Duhon Road walking towards the front door of the sanctuary. Before opening the door to go inside, I looked over on the right-hand side in the rear of the sanctuary; the roof was beginning to collapse, and the floor was crumbling. I remember seeing cracks in the slab.

Immediately, I awoke from my sleep and I felt the Spirit of God, so I got out of bed and went into my office to pray. I asked God the meaning of the dream, but I did not get an answer, at least not that night. As the pastor of the church, I knew the dream was profound; God was leading me.

Later that week, it began to rain consistently. And then, on Friday, August 12th and Saturday, August 13th, the rainfall was incessant for 48 hours. August 12th was actually the night of our annual youth banquet, and the theme of the event was from Hebrews 6:19 which is a passage addressing the anchor of the soul. The fellowship hall was decorated with a nautical theme, and we even had a life-size wooden boat as part of the props for the group pictures! The rain was so prolific that upon leaving the banquet, the parking lot was flooded beyond walking capacity. We needed to ferry the attendees to their vehicles with taller vans and trucks.

As we left the banquet, we noticed the drainage canal (called a "coulee" in Louisiana) next to the church quickly coming out of its banks. We never saw the coulee that full of water. What we did not know is that within a few hours, the coulee would rise to a record-breaking height, flood the church, the school, the Sunday school, the fellowship hall, a multi-bin maintenance shed, all buildings associated with our church (literally tens of thousands of square feet) and destroy nearly all the contents in those buildings.

The next day, Bro. Milazzo (our school principal) and I walked through the sanctuary in nearly knee-deep water. The water in the courtyard/grounds area where our school and Sunday school were located (consisting of pier-buildings and the fellowship hall forming a permitter) was up to our chests.

I was asking myself and directing my inquiry towards God, "Why? What was His purpose in this?" And then, I remembered the dream. I changed course and walked straight to the portion of the church on the front-right that I dreamed about and I found water going through cracks in the slab and undermining the foundation. Bubbles were clearly coming out of slab. I knew that this flood and all the events to follow were orchestrated by God.

This dream is evidence of God's faithfulness towards His people once again but, more than that, this was my personal source of peace. Because of the dream, many questions were answered before they were asked, many doubts were extinguished before they arose, and anxiety and worry were dealt with before it overwhelmed me because I knew that God was in this whole ordeal no matter how it looked to my natural eyes. At every juncture in the journey, whether it was a huge victory or when it looked like all was lost, I knew that all would be okay because He let me know before it happened that this was in His plan.

CHAPTER 2

FALLOUT FROM THE
GREAT FLOOD OF AUGUST 2016

What is a BFE? It is the Base Flood Elevation established by FEMA. The BFE is set from, among other criteria, the highest flood in the last 100 years. This is set as a standard to establish elevations in an area or region for all future development to avoid flooding.

In our case, we built our main sanctuary well above that mark and through our many years situated in southwest Louisiana (well-known for its wet weather and relatively flat geography), high waters never came close to flooding the interior of our buildings. The flood of August 2016 was not only record-breaking, but it also was considered a thousand-year flood! That means that an event of its magnitude has a chance of happening once a millennium!

Have you ever been in a rain shower that you could not see out of your windshield? Or have you experienced a storm that was so loud in your home that it scared you? That is the kind of rain that fell during this flood—for days.

The rain was caused by a low-pressure system that moved into our area and stalled out just northwest of us. The counterclockwise circulation acted as a vacuum picking up moisture from the warm waters of the Gulf of Mexico and dropping it over a large swath of southcentral Louisiana. It was ranked with some of the top producing rainfall systems in recorded history. This unnamed storm poured three times more rain than Hurricane Katrina in 2005. There was no chance of escaping it.

Along with many residents of our area, we suffered great damage as all our buildings were inundated with flowing flood waters. It was a sad day. It was shocking. It disturbed our lives and our schedules. We could not have church. We could not begin school (which was slated to start 72 hours after the day of the flood). Many people in the area could not access their homes. Families were displaced as they dealt with flooding in their homes and property. Roads and bridges were closed.

It was like the flood of Noah in that the slate was wiped clean and we were about to have a brand-new start.

This was the beginning of our journey.

CHAPTER 3

THE JOURNEY BEGINS

The first thing we did was begin the work of cleaning up so that we could resume as usual. We tore out everything that was visibly ruined by the flood waters. Like every other construction project that our men faced, they made a quick work of it! Within hours, the sounds of demolition filled the air. The bottom four feet of sheetrock was removed as well as all the doors and flooring. The altars and the pews were stacked against one side as the men worked on the other.

From a visual perspective, it was as though a bomb had been detonated. It was a mess. We ordered dumpsters and filled them up as fast as they could bring them. And then, after a few days, there was the smell. Floods produce a smell that is uniquely atrocious and impossible to forget.

Thanks to our faithful congregation and the help of men from our friends in Opelousas, Louisiana, Port Arthur, Texas, and San Antonio, Texas, the job went quickly considering the scope of the damage. It was while we were working one day that the pastor from Port Arthur suggested we should not try to reuse our old classrooms but buy or build new. The wheels started turning in my mind, but I never dreamed of what God was about to do! By this point in time, a disaster declaration had already been declared by the president and FEMA was mobilizing throughout Louisiana.

I knew that FEMA offered grants to qualified entities in our state. Not being sure where to start, I put a call into our Lieutenant Governor, Billy Nungesser. We scheduled a visit, and he came to see our buildings with staff members from his office, complete with state police escort and all! He made us a promise that day that he would do everything he could to help us to rebuild. This was the beginning of a great relationship. He and his office have helped guide us all along the way and we are thankful.

With the contacts he gave us, I told Bro. Milazzo to get on the phone and Internet and find out about grants that FEMA offered. Our inquiry sparked a flurry of events. The process required that we work with the Louisiana Governor's Office of Homeland Security and Emergency Preparedness

(GOHSEP). While the initial discussions with GOHSEP were encouraging, the months that followed were tough.

In part, our work ethic and commitment of trying to restore what we could worked against us because when FEMA representatives came, the initial appearance of the facility was that there was not extensive damage given all our cleanup efforts. However, what they did not see was the damage to the foundations of our two main buildings caused by so much water flowing through the buildings, not to mention the utter destruction the pier-buildings incurred from so much water saturation. The water even moved some of the buildings from their foundations!

For the church and fellowship hall that were built on concrete slabs, a geo-study would eventually determine that water made its way in and under the foundations and washed-out huge cavities. Because of this, the slabs began to crack and became unstable creating the danger of the buildings collapsing. This damage to the foundation was part of the dream I had at the beginning. At a glance, the bubbles coming up during the flood did not seem like much, but that would ultimately be a major factor.

~A Moment of Reflection from Bro. Milazzo~

When Bro. Schwing asked me to contribute and help with this book, it was very humbling for me because truly, in contemplating and rehearsing our miraculous flood journey, I have continued to be overwhelmed by the goodness and faithfulness of God. The experiences are still fresh in my mind, and to this day in 2025, I can scarcely remember a time when I have driven up to our new facilities at Town Center Parkway without having a feeling of thankfulness and amazement at all that God did to bring us from our location at Duhon Road to where we are situated now.

While I have so many memories, something that is vividly in my mind is immediately post-flood, I remember going into the sanctuary and looking at utter destruction everywhere. This was probably a week or so post-flood. Sheetrock was busted out of the walls, dozens of fans and dehumidifiers were constantly running which in turn, spread sheetrock dust and lighter debris, moisture was still very apparent, and the smell…what can I say? A uniquely putrid smell is part and parcel with catastrophic floods. It's a smell that is nearly impossible to mimic and just as difficult to forget. The malodorous smells borne in the depths of the devastating flood waters were inescapable. That smell…I'll never forget it.

Visually, tactilely, audibly, olfactorily, and even gustatorily—that is, seeing, feeling, hearing, smelling, and tasting—the sheer magnitude of the flood and the amount of destruction that were constantly present were surreal and astonishing. The experience of being immersed in such a situation bombarded each of the five senses. Life after the power and fallout of ravaging flood waters this close to home was beyond anything I had ever experienced.

But, my pastor has long preached on the power of prayer. Bro. Schwing is a praying man, and he has taught the church of the power of prayer. For years before the flood of 2016, we heard prayer preached hundreds—possibly thousands—of times in one way or another, and we saw the life of our pastor. He prays often, hard, with sincerity, and with a passion for God and people. He has a spiritual backbone of tempered steel, and I have no doubt that's because he is a praying man, and he's taught us here at ACL to do the same. Machines, tractors, materials, plans, work, and every other element of construction would be essential parts of the equation, but the most important element unquestionably was prayer.

And so, I remember going into the sanctuary that day. I was by myself at the time, and I looked around and really absorbed the extent of the devastation and what had happened. I thought about my life and experiences in God up until this point.

My life in God was forged and molded at 717 Duhon Road. I first visited church in this now-devasted sanctuary in 1996. We had countless services here. I prayed through here. I was baptized in Jesus' name here. I received the Holy Ghost here. I was discipled here. I was married in this building. This is where we had both Bro. and Sis. Broussard's funerals (in 1999 and 2014 respectively). This is where Bro. Schwing became pastor in 2000. This is where we brought our children after we adopted them. I had worked here every day at school since 2007. My wife had helped in the school since we came to God in 1996. This property was the centerpiece of our lives, and it was in utter shambles.

This is only to mention a fraction of the experiences that I had; there were hundreds of other people whose lives were centered around the house of God—this house of God, this place, this sanctuary, this holy ground, and our lives had been completely and forever changed. It would never be the same. Something in our universe moved, and that became very apparent as the days progressed.

When I went into the sanctuary that day and contemplatively looked around, I just began to weep. I felt so much loss; it's as if each broken fragment from the work we had done thus far represented a shattered piece of our lives.

And then, the preaching of my pastor rang true and very clear in my mind. Prayer works! His house shall be called a house of prayer! Pray without ceasing!

I nestled away in an obscure area, and I played "Made a Way" by Travis Greene over and over. The musicians had sung that song many times before the flood, but listening to it this time and in this context had a profound meaning for me. We were at a crossroads somewhere between our past, present, and future. We needed God in a mighty way. To this day, the song is still one of my favorites. The lyrics say this:

Don't know how but you did it, made a way.
Standing here not knowing how we'll get through this test
But holding onto faith you know best.
Nothing can catch you by surprise.
You've got this figured out and you're watching us now.
But when it looks as if we can't win
You wrap us in your arm and step in
And everything we need you supply.
You got this in control
And now we know that.
You made a way.
When our backs were against the wall
And it looked as if it was over,
You made a way.

And we're standing here
Only because you made a way.
Now we're here.
Looking back on where we've come from
Because of you and nothing we've done
To deserve the love and mercy you've shown.
But your grace was strong enough, to pick us up.

You move mountains, you cause walls to fall.
Through your power, perform miracles.
There is nothing that's impossible.
And we're standing here
Only because you made a way.

By this point in the journey, Bro. Schwing had shared his dream with me, and we were working through the early stages of the grant. The reassurance of the dream that God gave him coupled with that prayer meeting (and many more after that) were life-changing for me. I'm not sure how long I prayed that day, nor am I sure how many times I listened to that song, but after that prayer meeting, with confidence in our great God, His man, and His people in my life, I dedicated myself to whatever God was doing in the church corporately and in my life individually. The pillar and the cloud had moved. It was time to get beyond our comfort zone and launch into the deep of God's divine purpose and plan.

Weeping may endure for a night, but joy cometh in the morning! God was bringing us to a different place. It was time to work. It was time grow. It was time to get busy with firm reliance on Him and the church, the body of Christ, with the hand hidden under the wing—His wing.

CHAPTER 4

THE MIRACLES BECOME APPARENT

The dream, and the flood itself, were acts of God; He is sovereign, and He is in control. As events continued and our journey progressed, the mighty hand of God became more and more apparent. We began to document the miracles as they unfolded.

Some of the miracles are very granular and would require disclosures of confidential and/or meticulous details of our journey. That said, as the flood journey continued and we consistently saw the hand of God working, we became concerned that people would think that we somehow embellished or contrived these mighty works of God considering their scope. That concern, however, did not take away from our overwhelming conviction that these miracles needed to be recorded and printed as a testimony to the provisions of God and as a reminder to our posterity that God made a way where there seemed to have been no way. We will endeavor to document several of these miracles in this portion of the book in chronological order with details that illuminate the scope.

Miracle 1: From 1982-1992, all buildings on the property on Duhon Road were built completely in what would eventually be considered the current floodway

Floodplains designations are vast. When the buildings were constructed at Duhon Road, the floodplain was much different than what it would be in 2016. Flood maps change every so often. By 2016, the entirety of our complex was in a floodway as per federal, state, and local governmental geological mapping decisions. Because we were in a "floodway" and not just "flood zone," mitigation against future flooding was not enough; relocation became a necessity and an option. This forced us to look for another piece of property and to have an opportunity of receiving a FEMA 428 grant which is specifically for relocation.

At the beginning of this ordeal, we were trying to figure out how to build on our existing property. In the process of trying to squeeze an entirely new facility on a very limited piece of property, it became apparent that maybe we should look for a new piece of property elsewhere. Just as I began to drive around to look at what was available, an elder called me and said, "Bro. Schwing, why don't you build your new facility on another location?" This happened within a few days of the "floodway" determination. This was God's way of moving us to the prime piece of property that he had prepared for us on Town Center Parkway.

Miracle 2: Our school's official educational status

Our school was (and is) a registered K5-12th grade school in the state. While the affiliation with the church is part of the school's functionality and logistics, schools in and of themselves are classified as essential for FEMA. Had the school not been in existence and registered, there would not have been a prospect of a grant.

~Sis. Broussard~

This brings into account Sis. Broussard. In 1993, Sis. Broussard felt very strongly that the church needed a school. Of concern was that while the revival from without was exploding in growth (literally, a church was being planted every one to two years), we were losing so many of our young people growing up in church. Sis. Broussard felt that a central part of the answer was a school.

When the school was founded in 1993, it helped the church establish a place from early childhood through the 12th grade to teach children about God and academics. No one could have dreamed that the school would be the catalyst for being considered for the grant. Not only was the founding of the school a turning point for the young people, but it was also an essential component of the flood story.

Miracle 3: The flood of August 2016 itself

Catastrophic floods and similar events are called "acts of God." While the flood journey was precarious and filled with unknowns, the flood was an event that was miraculous in and of itself. It was an unprecedented, record-breaking event. Had it not been for the flood, and had it not been for the policies that attended to floods, this story would not have been experienced nor written.

Miracle 4: The president signs FEMA Disaster 4277 in August 2016, then increases the federal share to 90% instead of 75% a few months later

Most FEMA grants are 75% cost-shares which was the original amount of grant. That means that for every dollar considered to be eligible, 75 cents is given via a grant while the other 25 cents is the responsibility of the grantee. The president eventually signed a declaration allowing for a 90% cost-share, and then, only to certain parishes (counties in the other 49 states). This cost-share meant that for every dollar approved for the project, 90 cents would be appropriated via a grant! The difference in grant money that we could receive was categorically and quantitatively increased massively with this change. Our parish was included since the devastation was so extensive.

~In the Midst of Miracles, the Valley of Despair~

Despite all the miracles that had happened just in the first several months post-flood, this next event shook our faith to the core. We were like the children of Israel rejoicing to be free from Egypt and then, in a matter of a few days, we came upon the Red Sea with Pharoah's army closing in from behind.

Our Red Sea came into view on January 23rd, 2017, when FEMA sent us a report saying that upon their initial review of our case, we had "minimal damage." The memo basically said we could not get a substantial grant.

This was a low point that lasted the entire year of 2017. In fact, during all of 2017 and nearly half of 2018 we were in a fight that seemed like it would never end. Day after day, week after week, month after month, it was one set back after another. Several engineering firms did assessments on our campus (one report alone was over 130 pages long) and said that without question, there were structural issues with our buildings they observed that were extensive and grave. God had already given me the dream wherein I saw the cracks in the slab, and then, I personally saw the bubbles when I was walking in the buildings real-time! I knew those reports from the engineering firms were right.

To add insult to injury, we were told that the repairs we had done up to this point to have church and to continue operating our school were "permanent repairs." Think about it: All of the work that we did to basically survive organizationally was being used as a reason to stop us from a true rebuilding program. It was as if we were being penalized for our tenacity and grit. It was the hardest time for us. We needed the hand of God to help!

And then, in November of 2017, we were told that the only hope may be a determination from the local government's codes office stating that the buildings were "substantially damaged." Finally, a ray of hope, but at the same time, a grim reality. If the buildings were substantially damaged, and we had no doubt that they were given both my dream and the engineering reports we already had in hand, we would basically be homeless, and we still didn't have a substantial grant, nor were we guaranteed one. We were hewn in just as the children of Israel. There was simply no other way to proceed other than moving forward in that path and direction God had given me and that opened to us. We met with the city inspector in charge of issuing this determination and were told that we needed a structural engineer stating in writing, and signing off on a document, that the buildings were unsafe.

At this point, I would like to again remind you of the dream before the flood even happened when I saw that the front right side of the building foundation was crumbling. That would become so important during this phase of our journey.

The first thing the engineering firm wanted to do was bore holes in the slab and inspect the foundation and the soil under it. They came one day and placed cones throughout the sanctuary with plans of boring the next day in those spots. As I walked through that day and saw the cones, I remembered the very spot in the dream where I saw the foundation crumbling. So, I took one of the cones that was closest to that area and moved it to the spot that was in my dream. We told the firm that we wanted that spot to be bored for sure.

After the bores and drilling were completed, we waited for the written report and determination of damage. I don't remember exactly how long it was but to us, it was a long wait! And then the report was sent and we read the findings. They said that in and under the foundations were large cavities that were washed out by the flood waters, and it was unsafe for us to be there having church services or any other occupancy-type of activities. The report said that given the extent of the damage, we needed to evacuate the buildings immediately.

We presented the report to the city inspector and the substantial damage determinations were issued. We were not allowed to occupy the buildings anymore, and we were audited to make sure that we did not have any sort of organized activities therein. At best, the buildings could be used for storage space, but human use and occupancy was completely out as a matter of codes and ordinances.

This was the turning point with FEMA. Now that we were without our buildings, our case was back on track but this time, there were no buildings to work with moving forward. This ushered in a flurry of activity, meetings (addressed in detail in "Miracle 6"), our miraculous temporary school campus, and "the tent years." God did it again. It was another miracle! It was like passing through the eye of the needle. With man, it was impossible, but not with God. He is able!

Miracle 5: "HOW" the delays were God's perfect timing

We incurred delay after delay in our work with FEMA, GOHSEP, and so many other government and business entities. The delays were very disheartening. It seemed like we were being put on the backburner. Countless organizations and families were working with FEMA post-August 2016. The backlog of cases was incredibly long.

We called on a weekly basis minimally to put on pressure to no avail. We couldn't help but to wonder if this whole grant thing was only an unattainable dream. Maybe it wasn't going to work out. Surely there are time limits that we have passed. And then, it all came together in a few days, and we understood that God was in all the delays. That's where the House of Worship (HOW) memo, which was later passed as legislation and became official United States law, comes into play.

To understand HOW, the original scenario prior to HOW needs to be discussed. Initially, FEMA measured how much it would consider in its grants for mixed-use facilities based on usage percentages. That meant the school buildings were considered 100% use, but funding for other facilities such as the sanctuary would be based on school time usage. Since we had school prayer, assemblies, our awards program, plays, high school Bible classes, and other activities in the sanctuary, it was clear that the school used the sanctuary quite a bit, but not quite enough with those activities alone to meet the criteria. But then, there was also band class!

Allow me to explain band and its importance. In all the years of our school existence since 1993, we have never had an official band class with a certified band teacher to teach our children how to play all the brass instruments of a marching band, nor did we have formal violin/strings taught. With the idea of expanding opportunities for the kids, I thought it would be good for them to learn music for the future possibility of becoming church musicians.

This band class required an experienced band teacher. We found an instructor at our local music store (Lafayette Music). The band needed a place to gather, and the church sanctuary was the only place big enough! With all parts in place, the ACS band class started several years before the flood using the church sanctuary as its classroom. This became a major factor in the usage of the church sanctuary for the education of our school children. In considering the other usages, the sanctuary met the criteria of being part of the school campus and could thus qualify for funds. We were elated to say the least that the sanctuary would be counted at least partially!

That all said, the HOW memo was an absolute gamechanger. HOW was an executive order that President Trump signed after Hurricane Harvey (Texas) in 2017. A portion of HOW stated that if a church was supporting a school, the entire campus would collectively be eligible for comprehensive grant funds. Like many other FEMA documents, it was as if our scenario was used as the template for the official guidance. It was amazing because our scenario fit HOW perfectly!

Though HOW was signed for Hurricane Harvey, the memo also extended its effects to all other open and applicable FEMA cases nationwide. Remember, our case was still open because of the very delays that we were upset about, but the prolonged back and forth issues qualified us for HOW even though many organizations in Louisiana did not since their cases were closed.

Without HOW, and without the delays, the grants would have been worth about half of their final value. Over the span of a few weeks, HOW made our prospective grant double in value! The Lord did a miracle yet again!

MIRACLE 6: FEMA agrees on July 27th, 2018, that HOW applies and that our projects should be funded

We knew that HOW would apply to us as per several meetings we had internally, but without official word and signatures of FEMA representatives, we were still waiting. A formal meeting at GOHSEP headquarters in our state's capital city of Baton Rouge was finally set for July 27th, 2018.

Understand that we had waited for this meeting for nearly two years. Both 2017 and the first part of 2018 were incredibly tough. It was this meeting in July of 2018 that everything was going to move forward or come to an end. This was it!

We were on pins and needles for many days leading up to the meeting. The night before the meeting, I went to God in prayer and as I did, I felt a renewed love and vision for our school and church's mission which is to save souls and prepare them for a successful future both naturally and spiritually. So, I asked God to help us the next day in that meeting. I felt inspiration and began to type on my I pad expressing what I felt.

Bro. Milazzo and I walked into a room full of people from various levels of government. While we knew some of the officials, we had not met many of them. Understand that these were powerful decision makers who worked at very high levels of various agencies; what they determined would impact us mightily. For us, this was a MAJOR fork in the road of this journey.

A few days prior to the meeting, we were told by various parties that the meeting may not go in our favor. The state and FEMA were dealing with so many cases post-August 2016 floods, and there were many unique factors involved in each case, not to mention a heavy workload. There were simply no guarantees.

As we were all sitting at the table, I asked if I could start the meeting with prayer and an introduction of our organization and tell them of our mission. After they agreed, I began to read what I had typed the night before. The Holy Ghost began to move on the listeners. This is what I said:

I am Steven Schwing, Pastor of The Apostolic Church of Lafayette and Overseer of Apostolic Christian School (ACS). I've held these positions for 18 years. Thanks to all of you for being here today! I have with me here today our school administrator, Shane Milazzo, and our representatives from our consulting firm. Please direct any detailed questions to them.

Our church has been in existence for 40 plus years and our school is nearly 25 years running. We have served all social classes of our community. Every Sunday morning, we run a fleet of vans and busses into the poorest of our neighborhoods to pick up children for Sunday school. We love them, teach them, feed them and provide security for them by being there for them every week.

Our congregation consists of approximately 110 families and our school attendance fluctuates between 80 and 100 students. ACS is tuition-free, and all staff members are volunteer. Many are college-educated and are forfeiting jobs to work in our school.

It is our church's mission to be a place where people can come to know the love of God through their fellow man. It is the mission of our school to provide our children with an excellent education in a safe and Godly atmosphere so as to prepare them for a successful future. It is our goal to make productive citizens out of all that attend by teaching them to be examples of true Christianity.

We have existed on 30 acres of land just outside of the city limits of Lafayette, Louisiana. We have two main buildings: A cafeteria and an auditorium/sanctuary built on slabs, and 10 individual buildings built on piers sitting on slabs. We have used six of these buildings for school, and four for Sunday school. The cafeteria is used mainly for school and the auditorium/sanctuary is used 53% of the time for school and 47% of the time for church services. All our buildings have existed adjacent to the Coulee Isle des Cannes in what is now deemed a floodway although before now, it has never come close to flooding inside of any of the buildings.

In August of 2016, all the buildings on our campus were flooded with 8" to 20" of water. The buildings on piers were flooded with up to 20" of water and some of them were shifted from their original positions on their slabs. The two main buildings were flooded with at least 8" of water. Sheetrock and insulation were ruined, pews damaged, most furniture was ruined, carpet was ruined, and the slabs were damaged although we did not know to what extent until Monday of last week.

Not long after the flood [just a few months], we had a kickoff meeting with FEMA representatives and the 428 plan was mentioned; we said that we would like to go that route. It was also recommended by FEMA to hire a firm to assist us, and we did.

The following few months were a nest of activity for us because our whole operation was shut down. So, we did what we've always done...we got to work! We did enough temporary repairs to the two main buildings to resume operations. We did not repair the pier buildings, nor did we completely repair the slabbed buildings, because we were hopeful that the 428 plan would help us to build a new facility out of harm's way, out of the floodway and flood zone, and into a location deemed flood Zone X [non-hazardous/non-flood zone].

We gathered cost estimates, and then, a 130+ page engineers' report confirmed that the damage was substantial; we sent it all to FEMA locally. We then held a conference call several months later, and we were told we needed a substantial damage determination to seal the deal.

With FEMA's recommendation and guidance, we obtained these determinations on the 10 pier buildings. While "treading water," we continued to operate school and church, serving our community as best as we could. Our school was operating somewhat uncomfortably as we had school in the cafeteria which is only 41% of the space we were operating at before. Our church was having services in the sanctuary as before but many things in the building were not complete because we were looking forward to, and hoping to qualify for, the 428 grant. No complaints; just facts.

At the beginning of this year, the HOW memo was signed and deemed eligible for all those damaged houses of worship, and that included pending applications from the flood of 2016. In the memo, there was an example of who would qualify. It fit our situation to the "T."

Next, to qualify for 428 funding, according to FEMA, we needed to find out if the slabs of our two remaining buildings were indeed damaged by the flood of 2016. At that request, we hired a geo-technical engineering firm to come out and bore the slabs as well as the ground around the buildings. It was determined that our slabs were damaged by the flood and that our buildings were unsafe to inhabit. The firm found voids beneath the slabs and new cracking that was caused by hydrostatic pressure from the waters of the flood. After over 30 years of holding church services at this location, to the dismay of our congregation, our last church service was held in the sanctuary building last Wednesday.

Our first day of school is coming up in August and we have no place to hold classes because our temporary school building has also been condemned. We are currently seeking out temporary solutions as we wait to move forward with a much-anticipated 428 grant for relocation. I might note that the reason we are out of our existing campus is because of flood damage. In each case, at the request of FEMA, we obtained substantial damage determinations on the pier buildings and then, per the geotechnical engineers' report, the slabbed buildings were determined to be damaged by the flood and were not safe. All of this done in hope of obtaining a FEMA grant and to ensure the safety of the congregation moving forward.

As we sit here today, a clear picture of our entire campus since the flood of August 2016 is this: IT IS CLOSED! NO CHURCH. NO SCHOOL. VANS AND BUSSES ARE PARKED. FAMILIES WONDERING ABOUT THE FUTURE.

I am here as their leader to ask FEMA to consider our plight by moving our application forward and grant us funding. Our families have been in no man's land for the past two years and need some security in their future. Thank you for your attention and consideration.

I then began to cry, and I touched Bro. Milazzo on the shoulder so that he could address those in the room. Bro. Milazzo spoke with inspiration and passion. This is what he said:

My name is Shane Milazzo. I am principal of ACS. Late last night, I drove in from Pensacola, Florida for this incredibly important meeting. Nearly two dozen ACS staff members are there for annual training at the headquarters of our curriculum publisher. They are learning new policies, procedures, methods, tools of the trade, and the list continues.

Even now, as we sit here at this table, they are in various training sessions. They are looking forward to seeing brand new students who will be enrolling at ACS for the first time in conjunction with the current student body. Our staff is planning lessons, incentives, and effective disciplinary methods to maintain quality teaching and classroom control. They are members of the church, and they are moving forward in whatever way they can to prepare for the school year.

And yet, while we have eager families, freshly trained staff, the students, a proven administration, the desks, the supplies, new textbooks, policies and procedures, and strategic goals, we do not have facilities. The flood catastrophically destroyed our entire campus. The similitude of hope we had by temporarily renovating the cafeteria is gone. The buildings are uninhabitable; we cannot continue to operate in them and in fact, the local codes department called us after the weekend to ensure that we did not have services nor any other occupancy-related activities in the facilities.

As principal of the school, I am responsible for the daily well-being of our ACS school family, and within that responsibility is establishing an environment that protects our students and staff emotionally and physically. That is impossible to do at this point in any building that existed on our campus prior to August 2016. The flood destroyed them all.

For me, this meeting is about one thing: Being made whole. The two-year anniversary of the flood disaster is imminent, and not only are we not whole, but we are effectively homeless in every sense of the word. We need to be made whole. We have no facilities, no buildings, and no way of operating.

It is ironic that the theme of the teacher's seminar in Pensacola this year is "Building." Makeshift construction zones are used as props, and elements of buildings are often referenced in the sessions. While it is motivating to see, it is also a stark reality of how devastating our current situation is.

The spirit and letter of FEMA 428 plans, even documents that FEMA has published addressing relocation, fit our church/school scenario perfectly and categorically. It's as if our exact scenario was used as the FEMA-published guidance for 428 relocation grant funds.

It is time to build. It is time to be made whole.

At that moment, Bro. Milazzo also began to cry. After several moments of silence, the first words that one of the meeting attendees uttered were, "It's a lot to take in." After that, a few more moments of silence. The gravity of the situation was ever-present.

The meeting continued for hours with a plethora of interaction, questions, and discussions. While at the beginning of the meeting, it seemed that some of the countenances were hard and disconnected, the dispositions of all were softened and some were crying at the end. Our great God turned it around by touching their hearts and allowing them to see how we not only met all criteria, but how important this was for the present and future of our community.

We were told that they would do everything in their power to fund our entire project. But wait, that's not all; we were told we would get a temporary campus before getting our permanent work grant! In other words, we were told that we would get our temporary campus, we would get our permanent campus, HOW would apply to the grant, contents would be included, and we even qualified for a playground once we rebuilt (and we did; the playground was granted as well)! The scope and sequence of this meeting and the experience of being there and seeing it unfold is hard to convey in writing, but the outcome of it was truly monumental. Finally, we had a clear pathway forward. God gave us favor that day just as He has done for His people throughout history!

After the meeting was dismissed and we got up to leave, someone stopped us and asked us to sit back down. He told us in the presence of all the state employees, including the engineer, an attorney and others, that out of all the constituents they had dealt with, we were the most unique. We told them that we were God's people doing His will, and he, along with several of the others, said, "We know!"

One of the ladies spoke up and said that she had family in Lafayette and that when we opened, she was going to come with her family to church! God truly helped us in a profound way.

In contemplating this monumental miracle, these scriptures come to mind:

2 Corinthians 9:8 "And God is able to make all grace abound toward you; that ye, always having all sufficiency in all things, may abound to every good work..."

Ephesians 3:20 " Now unto him that is able to do exceeding abundantly above all that we ask or think, according to the power that worketh in us..."

Miracle 7: The TESI Tap

There was a concern we could not get sceptic for the temporary campus, and we could not do our sceptic via the old buildings since they were substantially damaged and basically untouchable. We also had strict building requirements as to where the temporary campus could be situated and how the configuration would work with department of health requirements.

And then, in the perfect spot, right where the temporary restrooms were supposed to be placed, we realized there was a 4" government-approved sceptic line where we could deploy an entire temporary restroom facility.

That 4" line had been put there, in that exact spot, in the early 1980s by Bro. Broussard, and it tapped into the TESI sewer system that serviced the adjacent neighborhood. That sewer tap had not been used for decades.

When we called TESI to get permission to tie in and set up an account, they did not believe that there was a tap in that location; it had been that much time since its last use. Upon inspection, they confirmed its existence and that it could tie into their system. TESI approved our use of the line. Without that tap, it would have been almost impossible to set up our temporary campus (which included the tent). Bro. Broussard was a visionary building lives and churches. That tap served its original purpose in the 1980s for a short period of time, and then, it served its greater purpose as one of the key components to our flood journey. It was truly a miracle.

Miracle 8: President Trump signs the Disaster Relief Recovery Act (DRRA) of 2018, three weeks before our posted deadline.

Because our buildings were sitting so high on their foundations, and because flood insurance was so expensive, we did not have flood insurance. Remember, until this flood, water from rain and the coulee never came close to flooding the buildings. That all said, because we didn't have flood insurance, we were penalized with substantial National Flood Insurance Program (NFIP) reductions in our grant funds. And then, yet again, another incredible miracle occurred when President Trump signed an act which attended to our scenario.

Organizations would no longer be penalized with major NFIP reductions. The law made any NFIP reductions on a grant limited to one campus solely and not divided out per building. Initially, before DRRA, we were looking at major NFIP reductions for the permanent work grant. Because of DRRA, the NFIP reduction ended up being a small fraction of its original amount. This was all done three weeks before posted federal deadlines; it was truly another miracle.

Miracle 9: Property at Town Center Parkway

We owned a total of 30 acres on Duhon Road which is where the flood took place. Approximately 60% to 70% of that property was determined to be either flood zone or, as previously mentioned, an entire floodway, and our sanctuary, fellowship hall, school buildings, and Sunday school buildings were in this floodway. These determinations disqualified that portion of our property as a site for our new buildings which forced us to look at a very narrow piece of land on the opposite end bordered by a neighborhood on one side, Duhon Road on the other, and a whole portion cut out by an underground gas pipeline.

It did not take long to find a very nice location about a mile or so away on a new road called Rue De Belier. Shortly after the flood, my wife and I and Bro. Milazzo went drive around and I showed them the property that I had noticed in hopes of somehow rebuilding. The property was listed by a real estate company and so I made the call. The owners were a family of siblings whose father had passed away a few years before. When they realized we were a church and school, they turned us down because of limitations it would put on the remainder of the adjacent road front property. They would not sell the property to us, but they called back a day later.

They said they had another piece that we may find interesting. It was not for sale, but they said that they would be willing to sell it to us. If it would have been for sale, it would have quickly been purchased by a developer, but God was reserving it for us! It was part of a much larger piece that was going to be a golf course, and the clubhouse was to be built on this property. That's right—the clubhouse!

It was the prime piece of real estate in that area, and it had large berms approximately 80 feet wide that both allowed for extensive drainage and that separated the property from the adjacent pieces. Along the entirety of the front of this property at Town Center Parkway is a serpentine 8-foot-high brick fence. The entrance onto the property has an arched gate on each side of the driveway. It makes the perfect entrance into the church home. The property had unparalleled natural and post-development beauty! We had another miracle!

Miracle 10: FEMA approves the property at Town Center Parkway and categorically excludes it from any archeological studies

FEMA grant requirements for rebuilding projects are extensive. Minimally, the property cannot be in a flood zone. Check! Town Center Parkway was not in a flood zone and as mentioned, the berms allowed for incredible water flow and drainage. While that was important to FEMA, that was also important to us considering our flood experiences.

FEMA grant funds also require that Environmental and Historical Preservation (EHP) studies be done wherever the grant would be invested. These studies can take significant amounts of time and money, and the results can mean a rejection of funds for building. An exception to this requirement is if the land was disturbed before the building process began.

Since this property at Town Center Parkway was going to be a golf course with ponds, berms, and sandpits, we had 18 years of Google satellite imagery showing the land was disturbed and even partially developed. Check! We were exempt from the study (which was a major hurdle).

Next was FEMA's approval. We worked with FEMA, EHP, and GOHSEP for months. Every single local, state, and federal requirement was met at Town Center Parkway. The prospect of finding property and moving to the new location was epic, not to mention that the property had more acreage than we anticipated without extra cost. The local government approved all zoning and planning requests that we made, and we were allowed to keep the beautiful brick fence (demolition at least of the entrance columns had been a possibility). Every single level of government approved our acquisition of the property, and all our requests were approved.

And then, there was purchasing the property. FEMA grants help with building, but they do not apply to land purchases. There is more on this in "The Miracle of Giving" section of this book, but suffice to say, we had the funds to purchase the property—cash! The property at Town Center Parkway was ours; we had another miracle!

Miracle 11: Covid19 and the school's contingency plan

Because of the flood, we created a complete contingency plan for school in terms of future operations and academics. In the event of catastrophes, our plan would allow school to resume remotely within 24 hours. We were able to launch the contingency plan when school was cancelled during the fourth quarter of the 2019-2020 school year due to the Covid19 pandemic and mandated protocols. Many schools across the country had no such thing. For us, we didn't miss a beat, nor did we miss one second of instruction time, all because we used our experiences in the flood to make sure we would be able to operate in disasters. Many of our methods were included in published academic research. God did it again!

Miracle 12: Temporary campus meets all Louisiana Department of Education Covid19 requirements

When school was shut down because of Covid19, aggressive standards were published and required during the mandatory-phased reopening in August of 2020. Because of these standards, certain buildings were disallowed from having school, and then, Phase I and Phase II guidelines restricted building occupancy to 50%. Our temporary campus was perfect; it met all criteria with minimal modifications.

The campus was comprised solely of "butler" buildings which all had outdoor access and no interior hallways. The school did not serve lunch. The school did not have a shared HVAC system. And then, our occupancy was perfect for Phase II guidelines with just a few small modifications. All these nuances were central to Covid19 protocols, and our temporary campus met all of them!

Keep in mind that we constructed the campus in 2018; it was almost as if we had Covid19 in mind during our planning because every single pandemic requirement was met! Several school administrators that we talked to across the country, even at elite schools, marveled at our campus configuration as we planned for 2020 with the Covid19 protocols in place. Who would have thought that we would be dealing with a pandemic, and who would have known that an outdoor campus in butler buildings would have been the perfect campus? Only God can make such provisions!

Note: We would not have even been able to have school in the old fellowship hall given the aggressive Covid19 requirements, but the outdoor-style campus was simply perfect. School started in August 2020 while many schools around the state, country, and throughout the world remained closed. It was truly another miracle.

Miracle 13: Vetting our architectural and engineering (A&E) firm

Because there were federal funds involved, there were many stipulations to follow in hiring the different firms needed to build. Going into the project, we had chosen Fusion Architecture without following certain FEMA guidelines. It's too long and detailed to tell how that happened. The important part is that we fixed our mistake as soon as we learned of it from GOHSEP; that included releasing Fusion from the project.

The issue was that Fusion had done quite a bit of billable work by that time, and the bill would set us back a good amount in our budget. The only way we could avoid paying it was if Fusion Architecture was chosen to complete the project per FEMA guidelines.

And so, we proceeded with publicly issuing a request for qualifications (RFQ) for an A&E firm that met all FEMA and GOHSEP requirements. The RFQ was even reviewed by government officials before it was published. A nonnegotiable date and time for RFQ submissions was set and part of the publication.

Bro. Milazzo and I had to be careful that we did nothing to influence the results. That meant that we needed to recuse ourselves from the selection process altogether. To do that, a neutral, eight-person committee that knew nothing about the situation with Fusion was chosen to make the decision regarding which A&E firm would be selected. Our church secretary sat through every part of the process and took detailed minutes.

The RFQ had a list of questions, and the answer to each one represented a certain number of points. The grading scale was part of the published RFQ, and each applicant was graded unbiasedly based on those criteria by each member of the committee. Examples of questions included: Has the company ever done work that was funded by FEMA? Is the proposal professional? Is the scope of work acceptable? Was the RFQ turned in on time? The list of questions was extensive.

Remember, because we knew of the outstanding bill with Fusion, Bro. Milazzo and I removed ourselves from the premises so as not to influence the results in any way. We were the only ones that knew of the situation with Fusion. The neutral committee was purposefully left unaware so that they could fairly and impartially decide upon the A&E firm. We could not, and did not, tell them anything.

Please understand that the chances of Fusion getting the job were very slim. First of all, there were quite a few companies competing. Second of all, a number of the other contractors were very well-known and reputable. Not that Fusion was inferior, but there was stiff competition. One of the companies that probably would have been a top contender showed up late to turn in their proposal and was disqualified. They were late because of a car or traffic issue, but a hard deadline with no exceptions was clearly established in the RFQ. Upon reviewing their very impressive proposal after the process, it was apparent that this too was part of the miracle; it seems they would have at least been among the top five and maybe even higher than that.

And so, the grading began. The committee members poured over each proposal, all the while grading the companies. The committee's reviews lasted almost three hours. Once the committee was finished grading, the secretary and one other person were asked to tally the scores.

Bro. Milazzo and I were in another room praying that God would have His way. When we were told that the grades were all tallied and a winner chosen, we went into the room where the committee was meeting. The secretary read the results, and we were amazed…Fusion Architecture won the RFQ by 10 points on an 880-point grading scale since each of the committee members had their own score card (each card being worth 110 points)!

As we dug into the grading, we found out that one of the committee members docked the runner up because that committee member noticed that the respondent would have been late on one of our posted project timelines. That committee member figured that if the A&E firm was late on that one thing, they may not care enough on our job to do it right.

God did it again! The results and details of the A&E selection were sent to GOHSEP and FEMA, accepted since all statutory requirements were met, and Fusion Architecture was hired back. We simply picked up from where we left off without losing one penny! Bro. Milazzo and I couldn't hardly believe it. It was so obvious to us that only God could do this. At this point, all we could say was, "WOW!"

Miracle 14: Bidding and construction at Town Center Parkway begin before inflation and Covid19

The bottom line here: The facility would have been much more expensive to build post-Covid19/post-hyperinflation. The delays in the grant gave us maximum grant money given HOW, DRRA, NFIP, etc., but we were just in time in getting construction underway to avoid financial impacts which would have drastically and disproportionly cost us significant money. The contractor and several of the subcontractors told us that the project would have been 60% to 70% more expensive after the pandemic but because all bidding was agreed to and signed, we saved that money! Bidding and contractor selection happened within a few weeks of the pandemic. The timing was beyond anything we could have planned.

Miracle 15: First service at Town Center August 13th, 2023—Seven years to the day of the flood!

As the project was ending and we were almost ready to move into our new church, we recognized the significance of the date. It was Saturday…August 13th, 2016, that the flood waters entered the buildings at Duhon Road; our first service at Town Center was on Sunday…August 13th, 2023. It was exactly seven years to the day from the day of the flood to the day of our first service in our new sanctuary! What a beautiful celebration it was!

To get a clear understanding of what we were feeling, allow me to paint you a picture. We went from having ALL our buildings and most of our contents destroyed to being in these state-of-the-art, beautiful buildings, in what seemed to be seven days, not seven years. Where did it all come from? It seems like it came from nothing. Our hearts were completely overwhelmed at the goodness of God!

To add to the depth of spirit we were experiencing that day, we carried our old altars which had been salvaged from the flood. Along the way in one of the services in the tent, I preached a message on soul-winning and how that we must carry souls to God in prayer until we see them come to God. At the end of the message, I had the men turn the altars over and the saints came during prayer and wrote the names of those they were praying for under the altars.

As we marched together from Broussard Hall to our new sanctuary, we carried those altars on our shoulders and placed them in the new sanctuary! Oh, what a move of God we felt that day! Surely our God, it is He that brought us up!

Miracle 16: The Boulevard
An answered prayer even after Sis. Broussard had passed away; a testimony of God's faithfulness

Sis. Broussard: "Bro. Schwing, when are you going to build my boulevard?"

Sis. Broussard asked me this question several times every year. She loved the thought of having a boulevard in front of the church and she wanted us to build it for our main driveway coming into the church. I always told her that since we had so many other needs, we couldn't build that yet. So, she prayed for God's provision of funds to do it.

On August 30th, 2014—two years before the flood—Sis. Broussard went on to her eternal reward. Oh, what an emotional day. She was our angel. Just having her with us felt like God's approval. She walked with God. She loved His work. She loved winning souls. She loved the church. When she went on to be with the Lord, she may have ceased living here with us, but her prayers lived on.

The day that I met the real estate broker and the owner of the property at Town Center Parkway, we walked through the old wooden gates they had set up to keep unwanted guests out, and my heart leapt when I saw how perfect this property was for us. We stood there just inside the gates as the owner explained to us the plans they originally had for the property and how those plans were forfeited by their father who had passed away a few years prior.

This reminded me of a bit of important information that I must interject at this point. One of our ministers was working for the father a few years earlier after the flood when I asked him to ask the owner if he had any property for sale where we could build our new church and school if we could ever afford to do so. His response was that he would work on it, and he would have a piece for the church one day. The father passed away before any transaction occurred.

Fast forward a few years and here we are standing on property that he used to own with a couple of his children negotiating a price for the piece of land where the church would eventually be situated. This property had no "for sale" sign on it. It was not actively for sale, but the son told us that they liked the church and remembered their father speaking of the church in a positive manner and they would sell it to us! It was just like their father said, "I will set aside a piece for the church, Pastor." God did it again!

Back to our visit at the gate: As we turned around to leave, they opened the gate and when we walked out, I saw Town Center Parkway—which is a boulevard—and tears came to my eyes as I realized that God was answering Sis. Broussard's prayers even after she was gone! There it was…a two-lane road with a beautiful grass strip right in the middle. We finally had her boulevard. Thank you, Jesus, for your faithfulness!

~PHOTOS~

The following section of this book is a compilation of photos chronicling this flood journey. It is virtually impossible to photograph everyone who was part of this story and journey, but these pictures are an attempt to both capture and convey the story as it unfolded real-time. Each photo has a short description.

Bishop John H. Broussard and Sis. Broussard

Pastor Steven D. Schwing, Sr. and Sis. Schwing

Sis. Schwing, Bro. Schwing, and Bro. Broussard

The Schwing Family

From left to right: My son, Steven, and his wife, Jennifer, with their three children, Ellia, Silas, and Ava in front of them, my son, Joshua, and his wife, Abigail, holding their son, Theodore, my son-in-law, Camron, with his wife (my daughter), Sarah holding their son, Kyzor, my daughter-in-law, Shelby, and her husband (my son), Daniel, with their children, Wesley and Everleigh, in front of them, and Sis. Schwing and I.

I am pictured here looking outside from the church foyer during the flood.

Our beautiful sanctuary inundated with flood water.

Our school and Sunday school buildings; notice that the light posts, fountain, and stairs to the buildings are almost completely covered by the flood waters.

I am pictured walking through the flooded sanctuary even as rain fell and the coulees/ditches overflowed.

A picture is worth a thousand words; the amount of water is truly hard to fathom.

Our fellowship hall: We had our youth banquet the night the flood began, complete with a nautical theme! "Which hope we have an anchor for the soul…" Hebrews 6:19. We even had a boat as part of the theme. It floated to the other side of the building. Incredible!

Bro. Milazzo and I in the flood waters.

"He turned the sea into dry land: they went through the flood on foot: there did we rejoice in him." Psalms 66:6

"Now thanks be unto God, which always causeth us to triumph in Christ" 2 Corinthians 2:14

Post-flood: We began the cleanup with prayer.

Busting out the sheetrock…seemingly endless amounts of it! The cleanup starts…

And it continues…

And it continues…

And it continues…

And it continues…

Signing the grant on October 31st, 2018, for our permanent facilities over two years after the flood and approximately three months after "THE" meeting with FEMA. When the grant was signed, we were overjoyed! We were relieved! We were excited! We had our temporary campus by this point, and several years after that, we would have our brand-new facilities.

The tent years…from November 2018 – June 2022. The tent is being delivered in this semi-truck.

Here come the school buildings!

Yes--it was a REAL tent!

Me, Bro. Jesse Broughton, and Bro. Rob Simon working on the tent construction project.

Bro. Patrick Simon and I working on the tent—several brethren, including Bro. Blake Richard and Bro. Stoute, are also in the photo.

It had carpet, A/C, heating, great lighting, and a platform!

Bro. Justin Regan and I filling up the first baptistry in the tent. The second baptistry was movable and heated.

We used every inch of space.

This is a view from the northside of the structure.

And did we have church—Wow! We did our best to reduce the noise for our neighbors, but the shout of the King was (and still is) amongst us!

Bro. Wes Broughton and Bro. Regan—The buildings had to be lifted nearly two feet higher than what you see here. They were all lifted simultaneously!

Bro. Milazzo and Bro. John Duhon are picture here. We have a saying at ACL: "Workers Together"

Cleaning up the newly built deck; the deck had a canopy and was the midway point between the five butler buildings.

A late night getting the temporary campus ready.

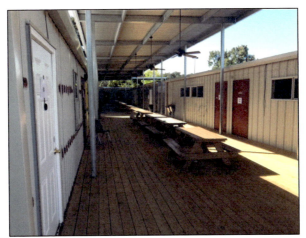

Ready for school!

Our first day of school in the temporary campus.

Assembly on the deck of the temporary campus.

Our students had the victory and maintained stellar attitudes. Our covered drive-thru area is visible on the left. The building in the background was for administration and the science lab.

This is the congregation's first visit to Town Center Parkway in 2019. Notice the beautiful brick columns on each side—those were there since this piece of the property was going to be the golf course clubhouse.

A photo of our groundbreaking ceremony.

All the men with shovels at the groundbreaking.

A photo of the personalized shovel and hardhat which was given to me at our previous appreciation dinner.

My son, Daniel, and my grandson, Wesley.
"One generation shall praise thy works to another and shall declare thy mighty acts." Psalms 145:4

We cooked meals at groundbreaking with our mobile trailer.

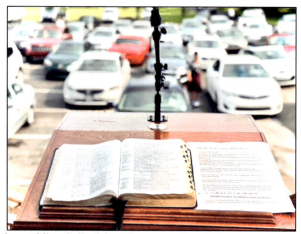

In the middle of all of this, there was Covid19. Here is a picture of one of our outdoor parking lot services.

We just kept on having church however we could! The platform was the deck of the temporary school campus!

The first of so much construction equipment arrives.

The first concrete truck arrives to start pouring footings. This photo captures the first concrete ever to be poured in our project; it's at the top of the chute headed into the footings!

The slab for the school is being poured early in the morning.

Men's workday in the school. Our church has many licensed electricians. They did all the electrical work!

Bro. Wes Broughton, Bro. Jonathan Richard, and Bro. Logan Broughton working in the trenches.

Bro. Jesse Broughton and several brethren taking a little break for some Popeyes Louisiana Kitchen fried chicken during one of the many workdays.

I am pictured under the concrete truck arch.

This is the beginning of the steel structure of the sanctuary.

The sanctuary at dusk in the early stages of construction.

Bro. Kenneth Richard doesn't stop!

The sanctuary is taking shape!

This is a picture inside the construction zone.

Bro. Camron Broughton has his hands raised to the Lord! He worked on the bricks around the steeple and on our tiles. Bro. Jesse Broughton and Bro. Corey McReynolds are in the lift.

Bro. Ryan Broughton and Bro. Drake Simon working around the windows.

Bro. Nathan Thomas, Bro. Thomas Roy, Jr., and Bro. Jacob Roy working on the landscaping.

Bro. Glenn Richard painting the church sign.

I wrote the following on the aluminum beams in the steeple. I am sitting in the steeple with it situated on its side before it is lifted to the top of the sanctuary. Immediately after I wrote this, the steeple was lifted via crane onto the sanctuary.

Note that the steeple of the church is built in the form of a lighthouse.

"Let the Light of the Gospel of Jesus Shine from this place! Bro. Schwing, 5/4/22 LET TRUTH SHINE!"

Our first day in our new school! This is in the atrium. Glory!

Bro. Milazzo and I doing the ribbon cutting!

Here come the kids! Sis. April Broughton is there with her camera.

Our new school and fellowship hall (named Broussard Hall) were ready over a year before completion of the sanctuary. We had church there. This was our last service in Broussard Hall.

The congregation as we prepare to move from Broussard Hall to our new sanctuary!

Carrying the altars from Broussard Hall to the sanctuary.

Please read the next page for the details of these pictures.

We carried the altars on our shoulders to the sanctuary.

"And the children of the Levites bare the ark of God upon their shoulders with the staves thereon, as Moses commanded according to the word of the LORD."
1 Chronicles 15:15

The entire congregation followed the men (ministers and leaders) who carried the altars from Broussard Hall to the new sanctuary.

The singers and musicians were in the sanctuary singing, "This Is Your House," as everyone entered the sanctuary for our first service.

The procession from Broussard Hall to the new sanctuary.

The procession from Broussard Hall continues.

Sis. Schwing and I entering the sanctuary for our first service.

Bro. Wes Broughton's smile speaks volumes.

A picture from the ground level during the first service.

Preaching the Word for the first time in our new sanctuary!

The first service was truly monumental.

~The following pictures of are of entire campus~

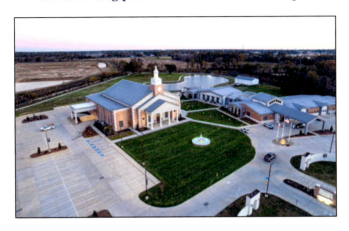

~Perspectives from Sis. Jessica L. Roy, a Saint, a Minister's Wife, Eagle's Nest Daycare and Preschool Director Designee, Mother of Six, and Grandmother of Six

My 40th birthday was on August 12th, 2016. My husband and I celebrated by spending a night out in a Denham Springs hotel which was about an hour or so east of Lafayette. Then it started to rain…and rain. We watched the hotel parking lot slowly fill with water and the sidewalks disappear. We watched someone driving a van try to escape only to turn right into a ditch when assuming to have found an exit. We listened and laughed to our own van honk its last breath under the brown waters that were slowly swallowing everything.

Water had entered the hotel now and the power was out. Dogs, the elderly, and some families who had sought refuge in the hotel from the last weather event that flooded their homes would all have to be evacuated by bass fishing boats down the city streets. I was having the most adventurous time of my married life! My top-notch husband being 10 years my senior didn't often welcome risk. We climbed up in the back of an old Cajun's dump truck on the final leg of our journey as we rode off to safety.

Back home, my dear sweet friend was planning my surprise party when she stepped out of bed and into water. Her beautiful home was flooding. Water was pouring in from her bedroom windows. Losing a lifetime of treasures and one's most foundational need of shelter is riveting.

Many of our friends' homes were being taken over by the unstoppable surge. All of these were the first to arrive and last to leave the church recovery efforts. There's a certain tenacity that comes out of tragedy. Someone posted a picture of the initial church member arriving to begin cleanup. The caption read, "The calvary has arrived."

First and foremost, the baptismal robes were washed. I knew we would be okay. When our church body moves, an overwhelming pride and security envelopes. We could go through anything together.

Next came the inventory. Every single item that touched flood waters had to be documented and photographed. Over 40 years of baptismal records, financial statements, printers, file cabinets, banquet decorations, pews, lawn mowers, and blowers were catalogued. The endless papers were starting to swell, and the ink was beginning to bleed. School textbooks freshly labeled and placed in student desks for the first day of school were ruined. The waters did not spare anything they or their humidity could permeate. Finally, however, our men got us back into our home sanctuary.

Yet, just as we were returning to a sense of normalcy, we were ordered to evacuate! I specifically remember the last night in our sanctuary that—as new converts 30 years ago—we had pledged to never leave. All I could think of was cleaving to Bro. and Sis. Schwing like Ruth and pleading, *"...Intreat me not to leave thee, or to return from following after thee: for whither thou goest, I will go; and where thou lodgest, I will lodge: thy people shall be my people, and thy God my God..." (Ruth 1:16).* And so, we journeyed—all together. Initially, Carencro's Apostolic Church opened their doors to us and reminded us that we were not alone. Then, a sanctuary tent erected on our home turf was consistently filled with His glory and that is all that really mattered.

Sis. Broussard did not live to see the flood or subsequent years, but her Grand-Souls and Great Grand-Souls did! One of the ladies she personally won by old-fashioned door-knocking in her later years invited a soul to the tent. She was born-again in that tent and lived for God all the years we were without a permanent sanctuary. That soul witnessed to her best friend while we were congregating in Carencro, and she received the Holy Ghost on a metal chair crammed inside the power-packed house! Bro. Broussard used to always say, "The deeper the cutting, the richer the cluster grows!" Both precious ladies and their children sit right behind me in our Town Center Parkway sanctuary.

We all have a book of miracles God has orchestrated so that He can build a temple in us where He can dwell. Bro. Schwing's vision for this entire campus spans far past our lifetimes. In January of 2025, he taught a message about preparing a place for Him—God is looking for a place where heaven can intersect the lives of people. Will this building on Town Center Parkway last forever? There is no way to know. But it will be a reminder to our children's children that you can build again. And it intersects this city's main thoroughfare shining a light on God's desire to see people saved. The Apostolic Church of Lafayette is a testimony to the generations of all to come of His true desire to make our lives His glorious temple.

Everyone has a story of devastation and rebuilding to tell. Whether the tale is of a life or a structure, it takes a complete walk of faith to rebuild. To be willing to let an act of God destroy everything known and to have faith that the rebuilding will not only happen but produce something stronger is simply otherworldly. It's like a trapeze act right into the abyss! Yet that is exactly what happens in the life of a repented soul who sees the need to begin again and places their feeble trust in His hands. The string of miracles that He does to help His child reach that broken place and the subsequent miracles He performs to finish the work is no less magnificent. The temple we prepared for His glory on Town Center Parkway is a physical memorial of the lives He has restored to carry His glory into this town.

Deuteronomy 6:20-25 "And when thy son asketh thee in time to come, saying, What mean the testimonies, and the statutes, and the judgments, which the LORD our God hath commanded you? Then thou shalt say unto thy son, We were Pharaoh's bondmen in Egypt; and the LORD brought us out of Egypt with a mighty hand: And the LORD shewed signs and wonders, great and sore, upon Egypt, upon Pharaoh, and upon all his household, before our eyes: And he brought us out from thence, that he might bring us in, to give us the land which he sware unto our fathers. And the LORD commanded us to do all these statutes, to fear the LORD our God, for our good always, that he might preserve us alive, as it is at this day. And it shall be our righteousness, if we observe to do all these commandments before the LORD our God, as he hath commanded us."

Some miracles are instant while the magnitude of others can only be measured by time. In this case, we were eyewitnesses of both. The miracles attended to the construction of the lives of people and the rebuilding of our facilities. All of it was miraculous.

CHAPTER 5

THE MIRACLE OF GIVING

2 Kings 4:3 "...Borrow thee vessels...borrow not a few"

It would be negligent of me not to mention the second part of this financial miracle. To mention the FEMA grant is mind-blowing by itself but that is not the only miracle of God's provision. At the end of the grant money, there was a delta; a lack that was impossible to meet given the financial status of the church.

At the beginning of the building project, I knew we were going to be short and so I went to the bank and opened a building line of credit. The bank gave us a very high limit with a decent interest rate. We were set. Every week when the bills would come in, I watched in anticipation as the grant money was depleted. I was ready to call the bank to get the funds we needed.

One week I called the banker to let him know that things were going as expected. We were going to run short of funds and I needed a draw. On the other end of that phone was a happy banker! I used the funds to pay the bills that week. Before the end of the next week, God had supplied what we needed to pay the bills of that week and to pay the loan back from the previous week. I couldn't wait to go down to the bank myself with payment to clear up that debt! That was the only time we incurred any debt, and it was only because of my doubt. I call it doubt debt and it only lasted a week. It never happened again.

As this point, I interject the following Bible story from the Old Testament describing what happened to us.

2 Kings 4:1-7 "Now there cried a certain woman of the wives of the sons of the prophets unto Elisha, saying, Thy servant my husband is dead; and thou knowest that thy servant did fear the LORD: and the creditor is come to take unto him my two sons to be bondmen. And Elisha said unto her, What shall I do for thee? tell me, what hast thou in the house? And she said, Thine handmaid hath not any thing in the house, save a pot of oil. Then he said, Go, borrow thee vessels abroad of all thy neighbours, even empty vessels; borrow not a few. And when thou art come in, thou shalt shut the door upon thee and upon thy sons, and shalt pour out into all those vessels, and thou shalt set aside that which is full. So she went from him, and shut the door upon her and upon her sons, who brought the vessels to her; and she poured out. And it came to pass, when the vessels were full, that she said unto her son, Bring me yet a vessel. And he said unto her, There is not a vessel more. And the oil stayed. Then she came and told the man of God. And he said, Go, sell the oil, and pay thy debt, and live thou and thy children of the rest."

It was God's provision of oil for this woman that paid her debt completely! As long as there were empty vessels, the oil kept running.

In our case, the offerings kept coming. God used His children, those empty vessels, to supply the exact amount we needed to finish the entire project. There is no other way to explain the unprecedented amount of funds that came into our offering plates except that God did it! He supplied the needs of His people...again.

~A Moment of Reflection from Bro. Milazzo~

The miracle of giving is part of the fabric of ACL and intrinsic in this building project and beyond. From the beginning of this flood journey, Bro. Schwing felt very strongly that the faith of Bro. and Sis. Broussard (note that for years, Sis. Broussard believed God would abundantly bless the church with money and resources), the decades of work of the elders, the church's vision for outreach, and faithfully giving to missions were key elements of God's blessings upon us. It was imperative to continue those things despite our own struggles.

Even though we were in temporary facilities, the outreaches and the church's cornerstone mission of reaching beyond did not stop. Initially post-flood, children's church was in the cafeteria space in the fellowship hall, and later, Sunday school was in shared ACS classrooms with children's church on occasion in the lunchroom area of the temporary butler building campus.

Beyond Sunday school, we continued knocking doors most Saturdays (except during major holidays and Covid19), home Bible studies did not stop, nursing home visitation moved forward as the church was able (Covid19 again introduced challenges especially in this area of ministry), and the outreach posts in Youngsville and two areas toward the northside of town (called Truman and Azalea) proceeded. These outreaches continued to be held weekly, and souls would attend the outreaches and come to regularly scheduled church services. Thee outreach posts are still operating today.

We also continued the Spanish outreach with both Bible studies and Spanish services. There are so many people from Central and South America in Lafayette and the surrounding towns. Having a Spanish outreach allowed us to disciple souls and have contacts in many places as we work in the foreign mission field here in our hometown.

We would generally have Spanish services in one of the school classrooms as we did for Sunday school. When we didn't have Spanish services, we would translate our English services for our Spanish speakers, and we still do that today.

The church also reached out farther from Lafayette. An outreach area was divided out and specifically designated for a growing town just south of Lafayette called Broussard. It's about 30 minutes or so away from ACL.

A group also began knocking doors in the Covington/Mandeville area when a couple in the church had to move there. Those towns are around two hours or so from Lafayette (if traffic is good) and through that outreach, contacts were established with families in the country of Honduras which has become a foreign outreach missions work.

More doors have also opened in the cities of Baton Rouge and New Orleans in that even now, there are active outreaches occurring weekly in those areas (an hour and just over two hours away from Lafayette respectively). One soul is worth the whole world. *"But if our gospel be hid, it is hid to them that are lost..."* (2 Corinthians 4:3). This is the Great Commission in action here in our area of the world!

But then, there are our partners in established missions overseas. For decades, ACL has faithfully supported the flourishing work of God planted by Bro. and Sis. Wheeler in East Africa. Bro. Schwing has consistently attributed the blessings of God upon our finances to a missions-focused and missions-minded mentality. That did not stop even when ACL needed money for its massive construction projects. The missions support continued, and if anything, Bro. Schwing established a goal of increasing it.

ACL also supports other missionaries throughout the world who are fulfilling the Great Commission, and several of us have been privileged with visiting a number of these foreign missions works personally. Even recently during a language school and mission trip to Peru, Bro. Schwing sent me with an offering for the missionaries. The missionaries said it was so incredibly generous, and it was exactly what they needed to finish out a headquarters hub of several churches in the Amazon River basin area. To God be the glory in both providing us the resources to support these works, and for richly blessing us at the same time.

Proverbs 11:24-25 "There is that scattereth, and yet increaseth: and there is that withholdeth more than is meet, but it tendeth to poverty. The liberal soul shall be made fat: and he that watereth shall be watered also himself."

There were also projects in other churches we fellowship which had various needs during these flood years. The men of God and people of God in these other churches have blessed the Lafayette church with their ministries, prayers, continued friendship with Bro. Schwing and ACL collectively, and with their hospitality toward us.

Bro. Schwing was adamant in helping these wonderful men of God and their churches even though we had needs of our own. The saints at ACL who were willing and able therefore packed up their bags and went to several churches throughout these flood years, helping with commercial electrical work, extensive renovations, construction, and yes, even helping with floods and hurricane cleanup that others experienced.

And then, so much work post-flood was done by members of ACL. There are only so many pictures we can include in this book. The talent, abilities, and willingness of the people in the congregation are simply remarkable. The amount of cleanup, construction, and renovating at the temporary and permanent campuses done by those at ACL itself is hard to fathom. Working with the local codes office, working with surveyors and with zoning and planning, all the electrical work for all the projects, the landscaping, the grand staircase in the sanctuary foyer, all our computer and networking infrastructure, reupholstering the chairs, so much flooring and painting, adding on another storage area (and the list goes on) was done by the local congregation. That doesn't bring to bear other church activities that were part of our weekly routines. The good people of God gave mightily; the miracle of giving just never stopped!

There is another consideration that I would like to mention here. Remember, very little had happened in terms of the rebuilding project immediately after the grant was signed. This was also when Covid19 was coming into full force and shutdowns were happening all throughout the world. There was a profound level of uncertainty as to what the future held during that time.

We were still in the tent and the temporary school campus during the beginning of Covid19. We had not begun the building project, and then, we knew that the building project would take at least a year and more than likely, longer than that given how vast it was (it ended up taking several years). Again, this was happening during Covid19 and the many aggressive ordinances appertaining thereto. But God was still in control, and He comforted us mightily.

There were a series of tongues and interpretations that were delivered during the tent years, and two particularly stood out both when they were given, and as time progressed. Both prophecies happened exactly as they were spoken in a relatively short period of time.

The following is the first of the two poignant tongues and interpretations given by Bro. Schwing. It was delivered during our service on March 15th, 2020, which is effectively when the Covid19 shutdowns were getting underway:

"Give and it shall be given unto you; good measure, pressed down, and shaken together and running over. The heathen will be broke but you will prosper. I carry you on

eagle's wings through this wilderness. You will behold the sepulchers of them that rebel—great things are ahead. Stick it out!"

And that is exactly what happened. While there were so many stories of tragedy and calamity all around us economically, God was blessing the congregation in many ways, including financially. Bro. Schwing alluded to the record giving that was occurring, and this was happening at a time when the economy was effectively shut down. Only God could have done such a thing!

The second of the two prophecies that stood out came in January of 2022. It said this:

"For I have seen your night of weeping, and I know and understand your pain, but I will have you know that joy is coming. I will have you know that I know your tribulation is long; your situation seems unbreakable, but don't forget who you are dealing with. I am the God that spoke this world into existence, I am the God that split the Red Sea for my people. There is a Red Sea ahead of you that I'm going to split, and this world is going to know that I am with you.

For you that are still here, there is a reward for loyalty. I see that you have loved me through the tribulation of this church, and I have purged out those who do not love me, and I will tell you that there is a blessing coming your way, that you will not have room enough to received it!"

Remember, when these prophecies were given, we were still in full swing of the planning and building project, and as Bro. Schwing noted, we were short of money. There was no way to trim the budget; the costs were set, and we were as lean as we could be. But our God is faithful, and after both prophecies in 2020 and 2022, God continued to work in this miracle of giving. Glory to God!

The final element that I would like to share on giving is this: During the tent/transitional years, we had 11 weddings for couples that stayed at ACL, and two weddings where one of the members of the wedding party was from ACL but went to a different church. In other words, we had 13 weddings that were either outdoor, in the tent, in Broussard Hall, or at another facility. We didn't have a permanent sanctuary! Some of the receptions were in a secondary tent that we purchased for events (and that we still use today).

During one reception (Bro. Schwing's youngest son's wedding), a very bad storm was passing through our area. The wind and rain were so powerful; we thought the reception tent might even blow down but wow, what a time! The more we gave, the more God blessed, even by adding married couples and growing families in the church. I can scarcely remember any other time that we had that many weddings in such a short period. How great is our God!

Truly in giving, we receive, and in losing our lives, we gain them. God abundantly bestowed upon us so much, and we did our best to give back locally, domestically, and internationally, for His glory. As Bro. Schwing said, the more we poured out, the more we received.

CHAPTER 6

CREDITS: GIVING HONOR TO WHOM IT IS DUE

Romans 13:7 "Render therefore to all their dues: tribute to whom tribute is due; custom to whom custom; fear to whom fear; honour to whom honour…"

There are a few hard-working saints that I would like to give honor. The first and foremost is Bro. Shane Milazzo. This man is incredibly smart and talented. From the onset of this whole endeavor, he has been to every meeting with his laptop keeping track of dates, deadlines, details, and other things I would have missed. The process of obtaining a grant is incredibly complex and not for the weak. There are a plethora of deadlines and reports to fill out as things progressed. He kept track of them all and had them all done and turned in on time. He did all of this while still running our school, starting Eagle's Nest Daycare and Preschool, teaching Bible Studies, filling in for me in the pulpit when I was out, etc. I could have NEVER done it without his help. Thank you, Bro. Milazzo. My friend. My helper.

Next, there are two men that were at almost every weekly meeting with the general contractor helping me to navigate and make decisions. Brothers Jesse and Wes Broughton. The sons of thunder that made things happen. Good job, boys.

Bro. Ryan Broughton: The all-round go-getter. He's on every crew taking care of anything he can get his hands on. Don't leave a blessing hanging around. He's going to pick it up. Thank you!

Bro. Kenneth Richard: The hardest working, most dedicated man that I know. Thank you.

Big Rob Simon: Thanks for always being willing to help. The staircase you and your crew built is magnificent.

Daniel, my son: Eager to learn and very supportive of my vision. We call him "Loyal D" for good reason. Thanks, son, for being there in the background standing with me.

Sis. Stephanie Hilts, our church secretary: How did she make it through all the complicated bookkeeping? We love you, Sis. Stephanie. God bless you.

The Congregation: This disaster could have been much worse. Besides all the destruction it caused to our buildings, it could have really torn our congregation apart. But I can say that through it all, God's children remained faithful and loyal. Proverbs 24:10 says, *"If thou faint in the day of adversity, thy strength is small."* I am a grateful pastor today because God's people have proven to be strong. I give you honor today for letting patience have her perfect work in you. Instead of getting bitter, you have gotten better, and that is because all of you saints really do love God. Thanks for sticking together through it all, and for all your hard work!

To the First Lady and my children (including my in-laws): My wife is truly a lady that loves God, her family, and the church. Through all the meetings and stress that I brought home, she bore it and was such a perfect partner to have with me through the journey. And to my children, I can honestly say that you are loyal and true to the cause. Thanks for standing with me as your dad and pastor.

To my son-in-law, Camron: You did so awesome on all the tiles. Wow! You made it look easy.

To all those men that worked on this project without tiring: Your reward will be great in heaven.

To Fusion Architecture: Our hard-working, kind architects out of Baton Rouge. Thank you for accommodating all the changes and doing a professional job....great job, guys!

To Southern Constructors: Y'all are an awesome team. You not only worked hard but you were our friends, and you always accommodated our wants...almost without complaint, even when we wanted to raise the ceilings in the sanctuary. Seth, thanks for taking good care of us. Todd was the perfect job supervisor. He took his job serious. As long as he had a straw to chew, he was fine! Hagen, you were a real friend and did a great job. Thanks, guys!

To Rostan Solutions: We never could have gotten this grant without your help. Thanks, y'all!

To GOHSEP: A huge thank you to Daniel Crothers, Danielle Barnes, Unmesh Kirtikar, Earl Ancar, and the entire tech team for so many hours of project work.

To FEMA: We are forever grateful for the efforts of so many and especially Eddie Williamson and Alice Jiffrion. Our recovery would not have happened without you.

We pray for all of you that God would bless yours for your contributions.

═══════════════════════════════════════

CONCLUSION

A PASTORAL MOMENT OF REFLECTION

Proverbs 3:27 "Withhold not good from them to whom it is due, when it is in the power of thine hand to do it."

It was right after we moved into our new sanctuary; school was in session, Broussard Hall and the kitchen were now being used, and the final details were being taken care of…we were all overwhelmed with thanksgiving to the Lord for what He had done for us. We felt so unworthy!

One day I went to Rouses Supermarket to purchase lunch and a man stood in the checkout line in front of me. I could tell by his countenance that life hadn't been good to him. As he swiped his card to pay for his groceries, it declined. He began to reach through his pockets in desperation so I told the clerk to put his and mine together and I will pay. Immediately he looked up at me with a look of bewilderment and said, "You don't have to do this." I said, "Yes, I do." I then told him of the goodness of God to me and how He has given me more that I will ever deserve, and I want him to feel and know His goodness, too.

I'll never forget the flood of emotion I felt as he walked across the front of the store and out the door. He paused for a moment and turned to look at me one more time and with tears trickling down his cheeks said, "You didn't have to do that." I don't think anyone else knew what I was feeling at that moment.

As I walked out of the store, the emotions began to build and by the time I got back into my truck, I was crying and telling God, "You didn't have to do that." I spent the day in humble adoration for the One that gave us so much that we can never repay Him. All we can say as we move on from here is, "Thank You, God!"

This short overview attempts to consolidate a seven-plus year ordeal into a very short record. It is simply impossible to convey the sights, sounds, smells, emotions, and innumerable life experiences of all of those who were part of this flood journey. God has not changed just as the Bible says. Beyond any of the untold stories is the reality that just as God provided for His people all throughout the Bible, God provided a way where there was seemingly no way, and because of His divine plan, we rebuilt a glorious house for Him and for His people. The completed campus at 300 and 302 Town Center Parkway in Lafayette, Louisiana is a testament to the faithfulness of God.

Without Him, we can do nothing, but with Him, we can do all things.

~He Brought Us Up~

Made in the USA
Columbia, SC
30 January 2025